In memory of

ROBERT D. MARSTON
1921-1980

Librarian at Bryan College
1950-1958

First long-term, professional
librarian at Bryan
and developer of
the Ironside Memorial Library

Given by his Family

THOMAS JEFFERSON
AS POLITICAL LEADER

JEFFERSON MEMORIAL LECTURES

Thomas Jefferson

as

Political Leader

By DUMAS MALONE

GREENWOOD PRESS, PUBLISHERS
WESTPORT, CONNECTICUT

Library of Congress Cataloging in Publication Data

Malone, Dumas, 1892-
   Thomas Jefferson as political leader.

   Reprint of the ed. published by University of
California Press, Berkeley, in series: Jefferson memorial
lectures.
   Includes bibliographical references and index.
   1. Jefferson, Thomas, Pres. U. S., 1743-1829--
Addresses, essays, lectures. 2. United States--Politics
and government--1797-1801--Addresses, essays, lectures.
3. Presidents--United States--Biography--Addresses,
essays, lectures. I. Title. II. Series: Jefferson
memorial lectures.
[E332.5.M3 1979]   973.4'6'0924 [B]   78-21568
  ISBN 0-313-20730-5

Reprinted with the permission of The University of
California Press.

Reprinted in 1979 by Greenwood Press, Inc.
51 Riverside Avenue, Westport, CT 06880

Printed in the United States of America

10 9 8 7 6 5 4 3 2 1

To Adrienne Koch

Preface

The three chapters in this little book originally consisted of public lectures delivered at the University of California, Berkeley, in February and March, 1962. They appear here without substantial change and with a minimum of annotation. That is, they remain in semipopular form and are still addressed to the general public. I have gone into the more controversial episodes more extensively and have annotated these more fully elsewhere, especially in my book, *Jefferson and the Ordeal of Liberty* (Boston, 1962), which was published after the lectures were delivered.

Years ago I set myself the task of finding out, among other things, precisely when and why and how Jefferson assumed the seemingly incongruous role of party leader. These questions have long been obscured by the clouds of political controversy, and the uncertainties of historians about them have been reflected in books until our own day. It has taken me a long time to get to this particular point, as it took him. In this modest volume I have sought to tell the essential story of his assumption of leadership and his exercise of it up to his presidency, when his circumstances and procedures changed. I venture only briefly into his administration in the final chapter.

Preface

Nowhere else have I focused attention on Jefferson's political leadership in just the way I do here, for I have been compelled to select the most significant strands in a complicated fabric and to overcome my reluctance to generalize. One generalization can be made without hesitation: that the period of Jefferson's leadership of the opposition is harder to interpret than the preceding years of his public life. I hope that I have contributed something to an understanding of him in the highly controversial role of party chieftain, and I am deeply indebted to the committee on the Jefferson Lectures and the faculty and officials of the University at Berkeley for giving me the opportunity to do so.

D. M.

Contents

1

The Road
to Leadership

IN CONSIDERING Thomas Jefferson as a political leader, we have to view him more particularly as a party leader. His services and successes in this role are of obvious historical importance, but we need not look upon these as his chief title to enduring fame nor like him best as a partisan chieftain. He is most challenging and appealing because of his diversity. He was a half dozen men in one and is endlessly interesting for just that reason.

Throughout most of his mature life he was a public man, but the patriot of the American Revolution who succeeded Benjamin Franklin as minister to the court of France was a high-minded public servant who avoided factional bickerings and whose intellectual interests were virtually coterminous with the world he lived in.

The Road to Leadership

In those years he does not look like a master politician, and one may doubt that he really does as George Washington's secretary of state. He could not properly be described as a politician in the common use of the term until after he became Vice President of the United States, in 1797. At that time he was fifty-four years old and had more than a quarter of a century of public service behind him. Not until then did he acknowledge to himself that he was the leader of a party.

After that, to a student of his previous career he frequently seems to be out of character. A question naturally arises. Was the party leader of these years of conflict which ended in political triumph the real man, or are these years to be regarded as exceptional? Leaving this question open, one can say that he appears to have become a rather different man. If anybody had told him that, he would probably have had an explanation. Early in 1800, writing to a friend in the West who had long been away from the eastern seaboard, he said: "Things have so much changed their aspect, that it is like a new world. Those who know us only from 1775 to 1793 can form no better idea of us now than of the inhabitants of the moon; I mean as to political matters." [1] Times had changed and, even if he was pursuing the same ends as

[1] To Benjamin Hawkins, March 14, 1800, in P. L. Ford, ed., *Writings* (1892–1899), VII, 435. Unless otherwise indicated, all references are to this edition. Unfortunately, the definitive edition of J. P. Boyd (Princeton, 1950–   ) has not yet reached the period in which these chapters largely fall.

previously, he could not follow identical methods. Circumstances would not permit.

In this period he emerged as one of the most effective party leaders in our history. How did this come about? The answer has to be in the form of a story which is in some respects familiar, but which can be freshly told. First, however, we should say something about what he did *not* do and the sort of leader he did *not* become. There are so many negatives, in fact, that we may wonder how he could ever have gained the devotion of a party and, during most of his years as president, the overwhelming support of the country. We must conclude that as a political leader he was so unusual that he may be called unique.

To begin with, neither in this nor in any other part of his career was he an orator who swayed men by public speech. Eloquence is not an indispensable adjunct of political leadership but, apart from military dictators, effectiveness in public speech may be regarded as the rule among the leaders of advanced nations in recent generations. Jefferson did little speaking except as a young lawyer and as a legislator, and he was better in committee than on the floor even as a legislator. He hardly ever raised his voice in public after he left the Continental Congress and entered into diplomacy and executive office. Even as President of the United States he made only occasional ceremonial speeches, besides his two inaugural addresses. He appears to have made no campaign speech in his entire life.

Though he did not often raise his voice, he did ply his

3

pen incessantly, with skill and potency. Yet, even as a writer, he rarely addressed himself directly to the public. The Declaration of Independence was a manifesto of Congress, not a personal pronouncement. Other famous public papers that he drafted were designed as legislative acts. They can be read to advantage but it is doubtful if they actually were read by many of his countrymen. Apart from the documents mentioned, his diplomatic papers were his most notable during the years before he became a recognized party leader. These were addressed to foreign governments or drawn simply for the benefit of George Washington or Congress. A number of them were made public and contributed to his reputation, but they were not directed to the electorate in the first place. He did not write for the newspapers during the violent controversies of the 1790's, though his major antagonist, Alexander Hamilton, did so incessantly and he himself was the target of repeated attacks.

While his reputation was largely based on his public papers, he exercised direct influence, especially in party matters, chiefly through private letters. It is doubtful if there has ever been a public character whose private letters are more important for an understanding of him. Some of his best-known sayings come from them, but in his own day these may have been known to his correspondents only. He wrote some notable letters to obscure people, such as students who asked his advice about their studies, but in general he exercised his influence on leaders. The most extravagant things he ever said were also in private letters, and some of these are

4

hard to justify, but he was no demagogue, haranguing the multitude and making rash promises. No one was more concerned for the interests of the people, but he rarely appealed directly to them.

He loathed crowds, loved privacy, and built his house upon a mountain. Yet he liked people as individuals and in small groups, and there are many contemporary references to his amiability—a thing which cannot be said about Alexander Hamilton or John Adams. He was generous to a fault, exceedingly hospitable, and had rare gifts for personal friendship, but no one would have supposed he had much mass appeal.

The whole field of human knowledge was his province, from the Anglo-Saxon language and Indian dialects to the bones of prehistoric animals. He had one of the greatest libraries of his time, and he himself wrote a book, *Notes on the State of Virginia,* a somewhat accidental work which in certain respects he had occasion to regret. Some of the most painful controversies of his career arose from things he said in it. His intellectuality was hardly as great a political handicap as it would have been a generation later, in the time of Andrew Jackson. There were other men of learning besides himself in public life; the intellectual attainments of John Adams were distinctly comparable to his. More than any other public man of his time, however, he enjoyed the favor of the intelligentsia, and his enemies tried to turn his scholarly proclivities into political liabilities. In the course of the election campaign of 1796 it was said that he was better qualified to be a professor in a college than to be the President of the United States. Timothy Pickering called him "the moonshine philosopher of Monticello." The most common charge was that he was basically theoretical, and in a sense he was. Few men in American public life have taken general principles more seriously; more often than he should, perhaps, he regarded these as universal truths. On the other hand, he had been schooled from his early manhood in the actual operations of government.

One cannot help wondering how such a man could have become a popular idol, if indeed he did before his presidency. In appearance he was rather unimpressive. Abigail Adams did not say of him as she did of George Washington that he looked more like a king than George III. His contemporaries described Jefferson as tall, loose-jointed, sandy-haired, and inclined to freckle. Apparently nobody said that he had a commanding presence. He was a superb rider but not the proverbial man on horseback. He did not become a national hero because of conspicuous military service as George Washington did before him, and Andrew Jackson and Dwight D. Eisenhower after him. He was an inveterate civilian with almost a phobia against fuss and feathers.

He did not have a conspicuous degree of personal political ambition. He was extremely sensitive to the opinions of others—which proved to be both a strength and a weakness. He wanted to be liked, or, to be more precise, he hated to be disliked. He was in the tradition of his own locality: he laid great store on good manners, and as a gentleman he sought to please. Although it was his policy to leave attacks publicly unanswered, he was not quick to admit mistakes. At no time during his career, however, did he crave power for its own sake. In this respect the contrast between him and his inveterate opponent is sharp, for no American statesman of his caliber, perhaps, loved power as much and sought it as ardently as Hamilton.

Jefferson was under no illusions about high office. He described the presidency as "splendid misery" and said that no one ever could hope to take out of that office the reputation that he carried into it. The charge that he had presidential ambitions, and was governing his conduct accordingly, was made by his enemies while he was secretary of state, but his most intimate political friend, James Madison, did not suggest the possibility at that time, and he himself undoubtedly found the very thought disquieting. Men like George Washington and Thomas Jefferson did not seek public office. The office sought them and they tended to accept it as a matter of duty. Jefferson's interests centered on his home, and it would be difficult to name a successful political leader who found combat politics more distasteful. The dislike of this amiable man of reason for personal controversy was little short of an obsession.

How, then, did he attain political leadership? The best quick answer is that he never did as many things as his opponents claimed, and that he became a national leader less by his specific actions than by what he was and what he stood for. His enemies claimed that he did virtually everything. The party line was laid down by Hamilton when the two men were serving together as heads of department under George Washington and the historic national parties were in their beginnings. Hamilton's partisans from this time on designated Jefferson as the fountainhead of all mischief. This interpretation was echoed by historians of the Federalist school; and in our own century, for different reasons, Jefferson's role as party chieftain was magnified by some of his most ardent admirers among writers and politicians.[2] Thus friends joined with enemies to perpetuate an exaggeration.

It is hard to say when national political parties began in the United States. The answer largely depends on one's definition of a party. The expression that Jefferson used at first and long clung to was "republican interest," rather than "republican party." The fact that he generally did not capitalize the word "republican" is suggestive, even when allowance is made for his penchant for the lower case. He hardly ever employed the word "democrat," which had a contemporary connotation of mob rule, though as time went on it came to be used almost interchangeably with "republican." He did not apply the term "anti-federalist" to his point of view or that of his friends at any time. The Hamiltonians applied it to them in the effort to stigmatize them as enemies of the Constitution, which they certainly were not, and historians have often done so unwittingly. Jefferson

---

[2] In Claude G. Bowers' *Jefferson and Hamilton* (1925), he appears as the party leader *par excellence*, before his presidency.

frequently referred to the Hamiltonians as "anti-republicans" or, what sounded more derogatory, as "monocrats."

Since we know how things actually turned out, it is hard for us to believe that there was ever any real danger of monarchy in the United States. The term "monocrat" may perhaps be regarded as a partisan exaggeration on one side, just as "anti-federalist" was on the other. But the American and French republics had emerged from a world of monarchies, and the counter-revolutionary movement in Europe was led by and conducted in behalf of kings. If there was a counter-revolutionary trend in the United States, as Jefferson believed, he would have had difficulty in finding for it a more fitting word than "monarchical." He used this until his dying day when referring to the political conflict of the 1790's. Repeatedly he described the monarchical faction as small; he regarded it as a group of leaders who managed to get into power but lacked a substantial following; he did not mean the whole body of Federalists but the group centering on Hamilton. Toward the end of the decade they were aptly designated as High Federalists.

His own attitude is characterized by an expression he used throughout this decade and which was conspicuously absent from the vocabulary of the Hamiltonians—"the spirit of 1776." The school of which he was always a devoted alumnus was the American Revolution. Nowhere, except in correspondence with his own family, was he so likely to be sentimental as in his letters to

9

Revolutionary patriots with whom he had served. Amid all the vicissitudes of party strife he never forgot his association with John Adams in connection with the Declaration of Independence. The simplest single statement of his own purposes in this confused decade is that he was trying to preserve the fruits of the American Revolution. By force of circumstance his role as leader of the opposition was predominantly defensive, especially in the domestic field. In international matters he was more on the offensive: he wanted to complete American independence, a task which was not really accomplished until after the War of 1812. Until his own accession to the presidency at least, he regarded the British government as the chief obstacle to the full independence of the young republic. To him freedom from the rule of the British also meant escape from their governmental institutions and practices. Not only did it mean republicanism rather than monarchy; it meant freedom from the sort of political corruption that was currently rife in England, and which, in his opinion, Hamilton regarded as inevitable in any effective government. The analogy of the American Revolution also helps to explain why, throughout his life, he clung to the terms Whig and Tory.

To his mind and that of his friend, Congressman James Madison, a trend inimical to the "republican interest" was manifest in the financial policies, political methods, and constitutional views of Alexander Hamilton. For his own part that brilliant and aggressive statesman regarded himself as acting in the "national interest." The issue, of course, was far too complicated to be reduced to any single phrase. Economic interests entered into it significantly, as they generally do, and in many ways the conflict of this decade was sectional. But there were about as many people south of the Mason and Dixon line as north of it at that time, and the overwhelming majority of the people of the country were dependent on agriculture. Hence Hamilton's critics had ground for claiming that they spoke for the popular interest.

During the early years of that decade, before he was in a real sense a party leader, Jefferson unquestionably rendered his most notable services to both the republican interest and the popular interest as a symbol. This may be said without derogation, for great leaders almost invariably assume a symbolic and legendary quality. They can hardly become great leaders if they do not. At that time he was an extraordinarily true and fitting symbol. He embodied the spirit of 1776 as fully as any civilian could. He was identified in the public mind not merely with the successful struggle for independent nationality and with anti-British feeling, but with the freedom of individual human beings from political tyranny or oppression of any sort. In his own state legislature, in connection with measures bearing on landholding, he had advocated the removal of artificial restrictions from the dominant form of economic enterprise; and, in his justly famous bill for establishing religious freedom, he had shown himself to be an uncompromising champion of the liberty of the human spirit.

The French Revolution was not a divisive factor in American politics for several years after it started. Jefferson reported on its beginnings with notable objectivity while in France. Most Americans appear to have viewed this revolution sympathetically, pleased that the French had taken up the cause of liberty after the American example and given it a new dimension. Jefferson's conspicuous identification in the public mind with the international struggle for liberty was somewhat fortuitous. His private endorsement of the first part of Thomas Paine's *Rights of Man,* and his implicit criticism of certain recent utterances of John Adams, accidentally got printed in the American edition of that work and led to a controversy. This was hardly fair to John Adams, as Jefferson himself perceived, but the net result was to identify him with the universal rights of man and to line Adams up, in the public mind at least, on the other side.

The contemporary of Jefferson's who did most to establish him as a symbol in the public mind was Hamilton. Angered by opposition to himself in Congress and by criticisms in newspapers, he charged Jefferson with being the instigator of it all. So far as actions were concerned, the man he should have singled out was Congressman James Madison. What the Secretary of State said in private about the polices of the Secretary of the Treasury we have little way of knowing, but he was far more mindful than Hamilton of official proprieties and stuck much closer to his own business. Nonetheless, in 1792, Hamilton launched against Jefferson a series of anonymous newspaper attacks which became notorious. The author of the magnificent reports on public credit and of the superb opinion on the constitutionality of the Bank of the United States descended to the devices of the reckless and irresponsible journalists of the time.

Even if he had had more specific grounds for his attack on his colleague than he did have, Hamilton showed deplorable lack of political acumen in launching it. He defeated his own immediate purposes for, far from driving Jefferson from a post the latter was actually trying to get out of, he occasioned Jefferson to remain in it longer than he had expected to. Worse still, he built Jefferson up in the public mind as his chief opponent; that is, he established him as a symbol of anti-Hamiltonianism. In terms of political tactics Hamilton made one of the worst mistakes of his career, but in singling Jefferson out as his natural foe he showed genuine discernment. There could be no quarter in a struggle between the most conspicuous early American exponent of governmental power and the country's most persistent advocate of human liberty, though in our own time we can learn a great deal from both of them.

Undoubtedly, after this display of Hamiltonian excess, if not before, Jefferson gave political counsel to his friends, especially to the members of the Virginia delegation in Congress, when they asked for it. But he did not need to argue these Virginians into a position of hostility to the Secretary of the Treasury, for, almost to a man, they were already bitterly hostile to Hamilton's domestic policy. What they did against this they would probably have done if Jefferson had gone back to Paris or remained at Monticello. His counsel to them in foreign affaris was more important, though this was largely limited to his special friends Madison and Monroe. Congress was not in session when word came that the European war had been extended to Great Britain; and the working out of the historic American policy of neutrality during the spring and summer of 1793 was wholly an executive matter.

The Secretary of State, though torn by his desire to help the French, whom he still regarded as his country's best friends and the champions of human liberty, as he still considered the British the major obstacles to the full independence of his own country, hewed to the line of fair neutrality with such success that he gained the plaudits of the British and even the reluctant admiration of some High Federalists. Rarely have American foreign affairs been more wisely and skillfully conducted. And Jefferson emerged from this trying year with enhanced prestige.

His direct services to the "republican interest" in this connection were rendered primarily by his private counsels of moderation. After he had discreetly informed his friends Madison and Monroe in Virginia of the incredible performance of the irrepressible missionary of revolution, Citizen Genet, who was defying the authority of the United States, Jefferson advised that he be dropped completely and that fair neutrality be loyally supported. Since the Republicans as a group had embraced the ebullient Frenchman with great ardor and had been stimulated by his enthusiasm, they were reluctant to abandon him. In this case Jefferson clearly saw that what was good for the country was good for the Republican party, and actually he well served them both.

When he retired from the office of secretary of state as he neared the age of fifty-one, he said and seems to have believed that he was leaving public life for good. Such was not to prove the case, but more than three years passed before he came back to the seat of the government in Philadelphia. During this time he made one trip to Richmond but otherwise hardly got off his own land; he himself said that he went no more than seven miles from home. Now, for the only time in his life, he personally directed the operations of his farms, turning to agriculture with greater ardor and delight than he had ever shown before. He set up a nailery at Monticello and viewed its relatively successful operations with intense interest. He wrote John Adams that when not on horseback, riding about his place, he was occupied in counting nails. He was writing few letters and reading few books. It was at this time that he started rebuilding his mansion at Monticello. What we can see there now is not the original house, built before and during the American Revolution; that house was partly torn down, partly incorporated in the second and revised version. The mansion house that we know, together with its dependencies, arcades, and terraces, was not completed until nearly the end of his presidency. But the process of demolition and reconstruction was going on in this period of retirement. Not only was he his own architect, he was his own builder. In the summer of 1796, which happened to be a presidential election year, he said he had one hundred forty men at work.

In these busy years of farming, nail-making, and house-building, he was politically inactive. The major conflict of the period centered on Jay's treaty. His opinion of this he gave in no uncertain terms in private letters: he regarded it as a departure from the policy of fair neutrality, as an ignominious surrender to the British, as a wholly unnecessary sacrifice of American independence for the sake of peace which, in his opinion, was not endangered, and as a major cause of both the foreign and domestic difficulties that ensued. But, in his own state, sentiment against the treaty was so overwhelming that his help was little needed. As for the tactics of the Republicans in the House of Representatives in their fight against the treaty, these were devised by Madison, Albert Gallatin, and other congressional leaders. He unquestionably approved of the conduct of the Republican congressmen, and undoubtedly he inspirited them by his moral support, but in no active sense was he their leader. The comments on public affairs that he made from time to time in letters are interesting and important, not because of any immediate effect they may have had on party policy, but because of what they reveal of his own attitude.

He now showed a much higher spirit of partisanship than he had while he was secretary of state. Out of office, he naturally felt freer to speak his mind, but the course of public events had much to do with his state of mind. Following Jefferson's retirement, Hamilton's influence in the government greatly increased, and soon it came about that no Republican voice was heard by George Washington. He and Jefferson had parted on the best of terms and there was no open breach between them while the first President remained in office, but circumstances were driving them in opposite directions.

The fight over Jay's treaty widened the gap which had already begun to open between these two great Virginians, just as it accentuated party feeling in the country. Washington's support of the treaty was incomprehensible to Jefferson, and to him this business, from beginning to end, was a Federalist party maneuver. Controlling the executive department as that party now did, and with a two-to-one majority in the Senate, it had imposed this hateful treaty on the House of Representatives, where the Republicans had a majority, and on the people of the United States, who did not want it. On the other hand, the attacks on the treaty were marked by violence, and in their criticism of Washington the Republicans overreached themselves. Jefferson became aware of this and, after the treaty fight was over and his side had lost, he counseled moderation in all references to Washington while he remained in office. But Jefferson was not critical of his fellow Republicans while the fight was hottest, and in this period of frustration he wrote his famous letter to Philip Mazzei.[3] In this he said that men who had been Samsons in the field and Solomons in the council had had their heads shorn by the harlot England. This was a private letter, addressed to a man living in Pisa and dealing with that man's personal affairs; it did not get out until after another year, when its recipient was so unwise as to give the political part of it to the press. At this stage in our story its importance lies in what it revealed about its author's state of mind. In its bad taste it was out of character, and it is excessively rhetorical, but it describes the political alignment as Jefferson saw it. No individuals were named in it, but it was a sweeping indictment of a group, and from its momentary lurid flash we can glimpse him at his most partisan.

During a period of personal political inactivity, then, his own partisanship intensified, and he became thoroughly convinced of its necessity. A few weeks before he wrote Mazzei, when commenting privately on the conduct and character of his unfortunate successor as secretary of state, Edmund Randolph, he had this to say about parties:

Were parties here divided merely by a greediness for office, as in England, to take a part with either would be unworthy of a reasonable or moral man, but where the principle of difference is as substantial and as strongly pronounced as between the republicans & the Monocrats of

---

[3] April 24, 1796, in *Writings*, VII, 72–79.

our country, I hold it as honorable to take a firm &
decided part, and as immoral to pursue a middle line, as
between the parties of Honest men, & Rogues into which
every country is divided.[4]

This passage, also, has to be pruned of its rhetorical
excess, but it leaves no doubt that he now thought the
taking of a decided party stand imperative. In this mood
he approached the year 1796, when the United States
had its first contested presidential election. With this,
however, he had virtually nothing to do. He did not
"run" for the presidency, for under the existing electoral
procedure nobody did that. It is hardly correct to say
that he "stood" for the office, since he said nothing
about it until after the votes were cast. His "nomina-
tion" meant no more than that there was a general
understanding among the leaders of the party in Congress
that he was to be supported. Madison explicitly stated
that he did not consult Jefferson beforehand because he
wanted to give him no opportunity to refuse.

In terms of direct service already rendered to the republican interest or Republican party, the person who
most deserved support for the presidency was Madison.
At the time of his own retirement Jefferson may have
assumed that Madison would get this support, as he said
he wanted this friend to. But for all his high intelligence
and devoted service, Madison lacked some of the things
that are most important in a candidate: he had not be-

---

[4] To W. B. Giles, December 31, 1795; *ibid.*, VII, 43.

come a symbol; he could not command the loyalty which the Republicans manifested so conspicuously toward Jefferson. Furthermore, he had recently been married to the incomparable Dolly; he wanted to retire to his farm, and as a matter of fact soon did; he was younger than Jefferson, and, while treated as a peer rather than as a disciple, he always showed his friend becoming deference. According to Madison, the Republicans determined to support Jefferson because he was the only man on their side who would have any chance of success. Jefferson himself must have perceived this, and from the time he learned of Madison's reluctance, he probably realized that he was doomed. He acquiesced silently in the inescapable.

In the campaign, if we may use that term, he appears to have done nothing whatever, except to furnish some information to friends who were defending him from attack. This campaign is notable on the one hand for the personal abstention of both Adams and Jefferson, and on the other for the scurrilous personal attacks on both of them. To Jefferson the most painful attack was on his conduct as Governor of Virginia fifteen years earlier, when the British invaded the state and put its officers to flight. He had been exonerated in his own state, and no charge of personal cowardice was made in 1781, as it was in 1796, since Jefferson was the last to leave; the legislators, including the redoubtable Patrick Henry, had fled precipitately before he got under way. But nothing could prevent these circumstances from seeming unheroic, and the echoes of these irrelevant ancient charges reverberated through the rest of his career.

Adams had an electoral majority of three votes over Jefferson, and the latter, according to the original provision for the electoral system, became vice president. He himself said that this was fitting, since Adams had always been his senior in public life, and that he actually preferred the vice presidency, because it would enable him to spend most of his time at home. His professions and protestations may seem surprising in such a good party man, but he had great respect for John Adams at this stage, rightly regarding him as a major obstacle to Hamilton's dominance, and there is no sufficient reason to question his private disclaimers. "I have no ambition to govern men," he said; "no passion which would lead me to delight to ride in a storm." [5] That was one of the things his enemies were saying about him—that he was no man to be at the helm in rough weather. He himself correctly anticipated the storms ahead. Not since the winning of independence had the international outlook been so gloomy, he said, and he saw no way to meet the situation until circumstances themselves should change.

No, it was not a good time to be president, and it would have been even worse for him than it was for John Adams. Diplomatic relations with French were suspended, and the great problem was how to deal with

[5] To Edward Rutledge, December 27, 1796; *ibid.*, VII, 94.

that nation. But the French minister, Adet, had intrigued for the election of Jefferson; and, while that gentleman himself had nothing to do with this, the memory of Adet's actions would have constituted a heavy handicap. If the French imbroglio was to be settled, it had better be settled by someone who could not be charged with being pro-French.

Jefferson's visit of ten days to Philadelphia for the inauguration may perhaps be called a honeymoon. He and Adams met on friendly terms—he went to see Adams, Adams returned the call, and they both attended a dinner given by George Washington. At that time both of them seemed relatively indifferent to considerations of party. For a moment it appeared that some understanding about foreign affairs might be worked out between them, but the members of the Cabinet, who were much more devoted to Hamilton than to the President, would have none of it. Perhaps no specific agreement could have been reached, but one of the saddest things about this unhappy administration was that Adams and Jefferson did not understand each other better. It is a pity that never again while in public life did they talk over the international problems of their country.

The net result of the election was to leave the Vice President as the recognized head of his party and with the prestige of having come within three electoral votes of the presidency. He had no rival in his own party, and the most prominent man in it next to himself, Madison, retired from the House of Representatives at this juncture, in effect leaving Albert Gallatin in charge of the republican interest in that body. Gallatin's abilities were of the first order, and his services to his party during the Adams administration would be hard to overestimate, but his foreign birth and French accent were a handicap to him in national politics and he was in no position to challenge the primacy of Jefferson even if he had wanted to.

Thus a rather reluctant traveler came to the end of one road; and a few weeks later, when the new Vice President, descending from the quiet and elevation of Monticello, went back to Philadelphia to preside over the Senate at a special session of Congress, a much rougher one opened before him. Then, after the honeymoon had abruptly ended, he found himself in a paradoxical and unprecedented position: nominally a high official of the government, he was also the undisputed and inevitable leader of the opposition to it.

2

From Opposition to Ascendancy

THE ROAD TO party leadership opened before Thomas Jefferson because of a combination of fortuitous circumstances. Luck is generally an important factor in the career of a public man. In his case, however, one can perceive also an element of fatefulness, a certain inevitability. If the basic issue was as he perceived it—between republicanism and the spirit of 1776 on the one hand, and monocratic and counter-revolutionary tendencies on the other—his whole past career predestined him to be the leader of the opposition, whether the post suited his temperament or not.

In his eyes the issue was unmistakable as between himself and Alexander Hamilton, but it was by no means so clear vis-à-vis John Adams, and in fact he had anticipated a decline in partisan bitterness with the accession of his old friend to the presidency. As for the second office, which he himself was assuming by grace of the strange workings of the original electoral system, he described this to a friend as a "tranquil and unoffending station." It would afford him rural days in the summer, he said—that is, at Monticello—and philosophical evenings in the winter, namely, in company with his scientific friends of the American Philosophical Society. He became president of that famous learned society, succeeding David Rittenhouse and Benjamin Franklin, on the occasion of his brief trip to Philadelphia to be inaugurated as Vice President of the United States. That was a very social visit; everybody called on him, he said. And the political atmosphere was amicable. But when he went back a few weeks later for a special congressional session, he found the situation greatly changed. Writing to an old Revolutionary friend, he said: "Men who have been intimate all their lives cross the streets to avoid meeting, and turn their heads another way, lest they should be obliged to touch their hats." [1] Thus it was in an atmosphere of animosity that this man, who claimed to prefer the plow to the forum and would have liked to be everybody's friend, assumed the presumably tranquil and unoffending post of vice president, and, by force of circumstances and his own past, the leadership of his party.

His explanation of the intensification of partisan bitterness was the rise of the war spirit when the strained

---

[1] To Edward Rutledge, June 24, 1797, in *Writings*, VII, 155.

relations with France became more widely known. Adams had called the special session of Congress because of the foreign situation, and his appointees as commissioners to France were confirmed at this time. Not until the following spring, when the XYZ papers showed that these commissioners had been insulted, did patriotic excitement pass into hysteria, but already it had sharply risen, and Jefferson's political enemies did not hesitate to revive the old charge that he was subservient to the French. This charge cannot be supported from his own records for any period; and there is abundant evidence that long before he became president he had arrived at the policy of noninvolvement or isolation which he was to describe in historic phrase in his first inaugural. He wanted to avoid the broils of Europe, especially European wars.[2] He privately recognized the gravity of the existing situation, but as the leader of the opposition he was impelled to play the dangers down. They were deliberately played up by the other side, and it is obvious that from the Genet episode onward the allegation that the Republicans were unpatriotic was a standard Hamiltonian tactic.

Except perhaps in a few wild moments, John Adams did not go along with this. In later years he was disposed to blame the partisan excesses of the time primarily on Hamilton, whom he castigated more severely than Jefferson did after the event—for the presumable reason that in the long run he suffered more from him

---

[2] In my opinion, that was always his position.

personally. No one can read the correspondence of Hamilton and his intimates during these years without noting the extreme arrogance and intolerance with which they viewed the political scene. This arrogance and intolerance must have been hard to bear, and the violence of some of Jefferson's private expressions can be best understood as an outburst against it.

Unfortunately, one of these private outbursts became public a few weeks after he became vice president. While on the road from Monticello to Philadelphia—while he was breakfasting at Bladensburg, Maryland, to be precise—he learned that his private letter of the year before to Philip Mazzei in Pisa had got into the American papers after several translations. In this, it will be recalled, he had described in lurid language the supporters of the treaty of John Jay with Great Britain which he so cordially detested. After translating the letter into Italian, Mazzei gave it to a Florentine paper; the Paris *Moniteur* turned it into French; and Noah Webster's paper in New York, the *Minerva*, published an English translation of this French version, along with some uncomplimentary comments on the supporters of the treaty and some laudatory references to the Republicans which the French paper had taken the liberty of making on its own accord. These were particularly unfortunate.[3]

In the existing international situation the publication

---

[3] The political portion of the letter of April 24, 1796, with editor's note, is in his *Writings*, VII, 74–77.

was sensational, and it afforded Peter Porcupine and the other Federalist journalists a field day. No doubt they believed that their enemy had delivered himself into their hands. This famous, or notorious, letter may be regarded as an offense against good taste. Also, it was far too sweeping an indictment and an extremely partisan document. But it was neither immoral nor illegitimate. Though it called no names, the Federalist journalists seized upon it as an attack on Washington, bracketing it unfairly with the diatribe against the retiring President in the *Aurora* a couple of days after he left office, and the abusive letter of Thomas Paine to him which this Republican paper had published in the autumn.

The Mazzei letter as it appeared in print was unsigned. James Monroe urged Jefferson to acknowledge it. The main reason the author gave for not doing so was that the difference between the published version and his own original would require explanations, that these would draw him into further controversy, and that in the end they would do more harm than good. Madison agreed with him and the letter was neither acknowledged nor denied. Jefferson got full discredit for it nonetheless. It did not deserve the indignation that was heaped upon it, then and thereafter, but from the time that it appeared in print he could not have escaped the allegation of strong partisanship no matter how hard he tried.

This episode illuminates Jefferson's methods and the allegations of his present enemies and later critics about them. His decision to say nothing about the letter appears to have been a wise one; it was in fact a continu-

ation of the policy which he consistently followed in this
period of making no public answers to personal attacks.
This also seems to have been a wise policy. It stands in
sharp contrast to Hamilton's practice of rushing into the
arena with drawn sword on almost any provocation. His
intrepidity and recklessness in this regard led him into
some of the most egregious mistakes of his career. By the
same token Hamilton gained a reputation for candor
and forthrightness which, in the light of numerous
private machinations of his, was more than he deserved.
But Jefferson's generally wise policy could be readily
interpreted as evasive—as showing an unwillingness to
meet issues head on. He distinguished between public
and private utterances, as one properly may, and he cannot be justly blamed for the indiscretions of his friends
—Mazzei's was not the only one. But his enemies would
not agree that he was a private man, even when in retirement. They claimed that he was conniving for the
presidency all the time. His efforts to keep personal
relationships above the din of political conflict, and his
proclivity to make things seem pleasant on the surface—
a proclivity which many have observed in Southerners—
these could easily be misinterpreted and lead to the
charge of hypocrisy.

In the eyes of the High Federalists, to be sure, he was
damned if he did and damned if he didn't. Five years
before this, Hamilton, writing in the newspapers as
Catullus, said that his colleague Mr. Jefferson had
"hitherto been distinguished as the quiet, modest, retiring philosopher; as the plain, simple, unambitious

republican"; but that he was in fact "the intriguing incendiary, the aspiring turbulent competitor." [4] Ever thereafter this was the image of their arch foe that the Hamiltonians sought to implant in the public mind, and circumstances conspired to help them.

The Hamiltonians clearly expected Jefferson to be the leader of his party, though they consistently called it a faction, implying that it was a group of disorganizers without real reason to exist. To avoid exaggerating the intolerance of the High Federalists we should allow for the fact that the concept of an opposition party was not yet generally accepted. That fact rendered Jefferson's position the more difficult. Fisher Ames of Massachusetts predicted that he would continue to pretend zeal for the people while combining the "antis" against the government. To this eloquent defender of Jay's treaty, it would seem, zeal for the people could not be real and must therefore be pretended. The Hamiltonians regarded Jefferson's early expressions of good will toward Adams as hypocritical, and they predicted that as vice president the "Virginia Philosopher" would have increased opportunity for "Jacobinical intrigue." [5]

[4] *Works*, ed. by H. C. Lodge (1885–1886), VI, 353.

[5] Fisher Ames to Christopher Gore, December 17, 1796 in *Works* (1854), I, 211; Chauncey Goodrich to Oliver Wolcott, Sr., December 17, 1796, in George Gibbs *Memoirs of the Administrations of Washington and John Adams*, (1846), I, 411–412; Theodore Sedgwick to Rufus King, March 12, 1797, in C. R. King, ed., *Life and Correspondence of Rufus King* (1895), II, 156–157; and other letters.

As presiding officer of the Senate, he was impotent in legislative matters. The Federalist majority in that body, which had been dominated by Hamilton from the beginning of his secretaryship of the treasury, was now two to one, and before the end of the administration became even greater. There were no tie votes on important matters; this Vice President appears to have broken only one tie. As a presiding officer he was notably non-partisan; and, by compiling a manual of parliamentary practice and leaving it to the Senate as a legacy, he made an unparalleled contribution to American legislative procedure. While he occupied this chair, John Adams had lamented that his wise country had fashioned for him "the most insignificant office that ever the invention of man contrived or his imagination conceived." [6] It may have been to avoid boredom that Adams entered personally into the debates and made long speeches, a thing which his successor did not do. Uncomplimentary things were said about the Vice President in debates, including references to the Mazzei letter, but since this was not read in the Senate (as it was in the House), he did not have to hear it.

In the House, where the Republicans were of approximately the same strength as the Federalists at the outset and where the influence of Hamilton was far less than in the Senate, the unquestioned Republican leader was Albert Gallatin. This he continued to be throughout the

---

[6] December 19, 1793 in *Works* (1856), I, 460.

Adams administration. What share Jefferson had in determining policy is hard to say because this sort of thing did not enter into the written record. The policy of the Republicans was to oppose all action which might lead to war; and, with the aid of the moderate Federalists, they kept military preparations down until the XYZ affair threw control into the hands of the Hamiltonians. Jefferson wholly approved of this policy, and no doubt he was consulted about it informally, but there is no indication that he sought to impose his personal will on the party leaders in Congress while he was leader of the opposition. Republican policy seems to have been a matter of consensus, and a high degree of party solidarity was attained in Congress. The Federalists spoke of a "solid Phalanx."

Besides being a symbol, Jefferson served his party at this stage as a rallying center, and by personal relationships contributed to Republican solidarity. He kept no house in Philadelphia as he had as secretary of state; he had lodgings at Francis's Hotel and during most of his vice-presidential term does not appear to have even had a horse. He lived like a transient, and in that time of partisan bitterness was a kind of social outcast. He dined every day with a group of representatives and senators whom one High Federalist described as a "knot of Jacobins." One of them was actually a Federalist; he found Jefferson's character "endearing" and some of his own party feared he would be weaned away. The capacity of this unpretentious Virginia gentleman for personal friendship was always one of his political assets, and he undoubtedly realized on it in these trying years.

Nor can it be doubted that he was a radiating center of confidence. That was one of the major reasons for his hold on his party. He described particular situations in gloomy terms, but his pessimism was always short-range; he was sure of the ultimate victory of his party because most of the people were republican in spirit, as well as farmers by occupation. That is, he was sure of victory if war could be avoided. As notable as his unshakable faith was his extraordinary patience, a quality in his statesmanship which has been insufficiently emphasized. He was an admirable leader at a time when his party had to wait and endure.

He served his fellow Republicans as a harmonizer and mobilizer rather than as an organizer. One of the first acts that signalized his assumption of leadership was his establishment of good relations with Aaron Burr, who thought that he had been rather shabbily treated in the last election, when as the second man on the ticket he had received a far smaller vote than Jefferson. Burr was no longer in the Senate but was a rising power in the politics of the crucial state of New York. At a later time Jefferson claimed that he had always distrusted the man, and perhaps he may have; he certainly had nothing to do with putting him on the ticket in 1796. There is insufficient reason, however, to think that Burr was a widely distrusted person at this time. It may even be said that Hamilton was under a darker cloud in the early part of the Adams administration, for it was in the summer and autumn of 1797 that the famous Reynolds (Mrs. Reynolds) scandal broke into the open. At any rate, Jefferson as a realistic politician wanted his party to thrive in New York. His advances, by letter, caused Burr to come to Philadelphia to see him. Burr's arrival fortunately coincided with that of James Monroe from France. Since Monroe was in political trouble—the Federalists regarded him as disgraced—a council of war was in order. Jefferson, Gallatin, Burr, and Monroe conferred, and thus the inner circle of Republican leaders was reformed except for Madison—who, however, was kept in touch with the course of events by his friend the Vice President.

Jefferson's loyal support of Monroe in his troubles might have been expected on personal grounds, but it suggests another reason for his hold on his party. He was loyal to and essentially uncritical of anyone with whom he was in basic political agreement. Individualist though he was, he was a good party man. His relations with Burr also suggest more than that politics makes strange bedfellows. Outside his own state, he played no direct part in local politics except as an encourager, and this was true most of the time even in Virginia. He left management to the people on the ground, in whom he reposed full confidence. He has been described as an easy boss, but it would be more accurate to say that he did not permit his followers to think of him as a boss at all. Here, again, the contrast with Hamilton is striking. Hamilton, whose military talents and proclivities were pronounced, was a political commander; Jefferson, the inveterate civilian, was a leader.

In those days of painfully slow transportation, personal communication had to be by letters to an extent which is hard for us to realize. Jefferson was generally a prolific letter writer, but his only regular correspondence while at the seat of government was with Madison and with members of his own family. Rarely did he take the initiative in this period: nearly all his political letters were in response to those he received from others. His letters did not deal with public affairs alone, but he took advantage of his opportunities to set forth his view of things. This may be designated as the Republican view, for he was the spokesman of his party if anybody was and he well knew the sentiments of Gallatin and other leaders in Philadelphia. At first he did not hesitate to make these views known to men whom he regarded as moderates and sought to woo—most notably to Adams's friend Elbridge Gerry, who became the third member of the ill-fated commission to France. But the Vice President was in no position to influence the course of diplomatic negotiations, and circumstances made it increasingly difficult to present his views, on either foreign or domestic issues, outside of Republican circles. In writing to persons who were unquestionably of his own persuasion he sought to be informative and stimulating, and he became more and more critical of the administration.

In view of what had happened to his letter to Mazzei it is not surprising that he often warned his correspondents not to let what he wrote them privately get into the papers. Willful abuses of his confidence were relatively rare, but comments of his on public affairs circulated among Republicans, as no doubt he hoped they would, and some of them came in distorted form to ears for which they were not intended. A good example was provided by a letter he wrote a Maryland planter, Peregrine Fitzhugh, soon after his return to the seat of government. In this he commented on the President's purposes in calling the special session of Congress, in effect identifying him with the "war party." This interpretation was unjust to Adams, though we must recognize that Jefferson could not read Adams's letters as we can, and that after the first few days the President never explained his position to Jefferson.

Fitzhugh communicated the contents of the letter to several good Republicans, and news of it eventually reached the Federalists, who proceeded to spread exaggerated reports. Desiring to correct these exaggerations, Fitzhugh unwisely showed the letter to a Federalist kinsman. This gentleman, Uriah Forrest, then proceeded to write down its substance from memory and sent it in this form to Adams, warning him to be on his guard and at the same time asking him not to give away his own abuse of confidence. No breach between Adams and Jefferson had previously been avowed, but this bizarre episode marks one, even though it did not get into the open. The paper, Adams said, was "evidence of a mind soured, yet seeking for popularity, and eaten to a honeycomb with ambition, yet weak, confused, uninformed, and ignorant. I have been long convinced that this ambition is so inconsiderate as to be capable of going great lengths." Adams had ground for annoyance, but he let his vanity run away with his judgment.[7]

Some distinction should be made between the first year of the Adams administration, when after a brief period of amicability the Republican situation was bad, and the period following the XYZ disclosures, when it was much worse. The patriotic hysteria occasioned by the revelation of French insults to the American commissioners and the full severance of diplomatic relations declined somewhat after another year; and by the election year of 1800 the Federalists, caught in the toils of their own excesses, were rent by dissension. By that time, also, Adams had wisely instituted the negotiations which eventually removed the French issue from American politics, despite the frantic effort of the Hamiltonians to keep it there. It was during the darkest and most dangerous months that Jefferson performed his most significant services as a party leader, concealing his actions to a degree that he had never done before and was never to do again.

After the XYZ disclosures the position of the Republicans was precarious. Circumstances had played into the hands of the High Federalists, who really constituted the

---

[7] Adams to Forrest, June 20, 1797, in *Works*, VIII, 546–547. Jefferson's letter of June 4, 1797 to Fitzhugh is in his *Writings*, VII, 134–138, and letters from Fitzhugh to Jefferson, and Forrest to Adams, are in the Jefferson and Adams Papers.

war party. Adams himself seemed to be caught up in the war fever, and John Marshall, the first of the commissioners to get home from France, was greeted as a conquering hero. During that mad time Jefferson could do nothing to affect the course of events, and the Republicans in Congress could do no more than hang on. He was convinced that the French did not want war, a judgment which history confirmed. In his private comments he put the best face he could on the foolish actions of the French, being less critical than he might have been, and he made some criticisms of American procedure which seem warranted. But to say these things publicly would have been to be labeled as unpatriotic and to serve no immediate purpose. The basic errors in foreign policy which had brought this situation about could not be speedily undone. The only thing the Republicans in Congress could do was to try to prevent precipitate action.

Despite his apparent impotence, Jefferson looked back on his services to his party and his country during the notorious XYZ Congress as among the most important in his career. He said this in connection with the pathetic account of his public life, in his last year, when he was in financial distress and was arguing the propriety of a lottery for his benefit. Despite the long lapse of time he correctly described the state of affairs.[8] Despairing of the situation in Philadelphia, a number of Republican

---

[8] February, 1826, in *Writings*, X, 368–369.

congressional leaders went home to mend their political fences there, believing that effective opposition to the policies of the federal government would henceforth have to center on the states. Weakened by these withdrawals, the Republican minority were threatened with apathy and despair. In Jefferson's own opinion, he and Gallatin shared the task of keeping them alive. Perhaps we shall never know in detail just how he did his part, but obviously he was a rallying center and a morale builder. He could not check the legislative course of the extreme Federalists, who were now in the saddle and riding hard, but he undoubtedly played a crucial role in the preservation of the party of the opposition. And this he did more by reason of his character, personality, and basic philosophy than by any specific action.

It need not be supposed that the Republicans and their leaders were always right in their attitude toward specific measures. For example, John Adams was more far-sighted than they in starting a navy. But they were clearly right in their judgment that the dangers of the hour were exaggerated. And they correctly foresaw that there would be strenuous objection to the increase in taxes when the people began to doubt the seriousness of the crisis. In pressing this point Jefferson showed himself to be an astute politician, but he and his party gain their chief merit in history for their opposition to the measures which bore most directly on human liberty and pointed toward what we now call the police state. One was the creation of an unnecessarily large army which, in effect, would have been under Hamilton's command.

Since there never was any likelihood that such a force would be needed to repel a French invasion, historians have properly asked what its foreseeable uses could have been. One possibility was that it could have been used in an imperialistic adventure to the southward, against the Spanish and in conjunction with the British. In view of the inflexible opposition of John Adams to this, as well as other unfavorable circumstances, it was only a remote possibility. Jefferson referred to Hamilton at least once as a prospective Bonaparte, but his greater fear was that an expanded army would be used to crush domestic political opposition on the pretext of putting down insurrection. That Hamilton and his devotees would have welcomed the opportunity to employ military force for such a purpose can hardly be questioned in view of what they wrote each other. Credit for blocking the military designs of the High Federalists must be given Adams, and it is a pity that he and his old friend Jefferson did not understand each other better in this matter. But Jefferson sensed the realities from the beginning, and he and his party put themselves on record against a degree of militarism which was intrinsically undesirable and for which there was no demonstrable need.

The Alien and Sedition Acts represented a greater and more immediate challenge to human freedom and the right of political opposition; it will be discussed in the final chapter. At this point, we may consider the repressive effect of these various measures and of the atmosphere of the time on Jefferson and his own methods.

The effect was certainly not to quench his spirit, but it was to limit his activities, to silence and immobilize him in public. To a greater extent than ever before he had to depend on others, and he served chiefly as a catalytic agent. This was more than a question of personal prudence. His intimates realized as fully as he that it would be a disaster to his party and to the cause of freedom he embodied if he were publicly discredited.

The difficulties of his position were immense, and his conduct must be viewed in the light of them. It is a matter of mere speculation whether he might have been impeached, since he saw to it that there was no occasion to proceed against him. In this period he drew several sets of resolutions, highly critical of policies of the government, which became part of the public record, the most important being the Kentucky Resolutions of 1798, but these were presented in the names of others. We may not like this secret procedure, but if he was going to oppose the administration it is hard to see how else he could have done it. We are safe in assuming that he did not write under a pseudonym for the newspapers. He left to his friends the defense of him against attack and they needed no urging. He himself was very active in distributing pamphlets written by others, and upon occasion he urged persons who thought as he did to take up the issues of the day in pamphlets or newspapers. Among these was his old colleague, Edmund Pendleton. Lest it be thought that the prudent Jefferson encouraged others to undergo risks he himself was avoiding, it may be added that this highly esteemed Virginia judge involved himself in no peril by responding. And the encouragement Jefferson gave Republican newspapermen involved them in no dangers they did not face already. In this period, more than ever before, he restricted and guarded his private letters. Repeatedly he told Madison and Monroe that he would not write them often. He asked them to make a practice of examining the seals on his letters to see if they had been opened, and, judging from what others besides him said, his suspicions were well founded. It was easier to open letters before the age of envelopes. Distrusting the postal service, he often held up an important letter until he could find that some reliable person could deliver it.

He may never have found out that one private letter to him—from the American Consul General in Paris—was commandeered by Secretary of the Treasury Wolcott under circumstances that suggest a detective story.[9] In pursuit of wild rumors of treasonable correspondence, Wolcott went to New York and obtained this letter from the gentleman who bore it, with others, from France. It now seems innocuous, and at the worst Jefferson could only have been charged with guilt by association. Perhaps the assiduous Secretary of the Treasury concluded he could not really do much with it;

---

[9] From Fulwar Skipwith, March 17, 1798. The letter was published in George Gibbs, *Memoirs of the Administrations of Washington and John Adams* (1846), II, 158–161, from the Wolcott Papers in Hartford, Connecticut, where it still is.

perhaps he kept it up his sleeve for some future contingency.

Jefferson had occasional letters from France in these years, but he said that he stopped writing to his friends there when he retired from the secretaryship of state, except for his old secretary, William Short, and James Monroe when in that country. There is no reason to doubt the accuracy of this statement. Nevertheless, rumors ran around Philadelphia that he was engaged in traitorous correspondence with Talleyrand and members of the Directory. One variation of this charge was that he gave letters to Dr. George Logan, who went abroad as a self-appointed crusader for international peace, becoming a highly controversial figure in consequence. Jefferson did give him a letter affirming his citizenship and character, and approved of him as a good Republican and friend of peace, but he kept his hands clean in this and other international matters.

For him this continued to be a time, primarily, of watchful waiting for some change in the international situation, waiting for hysteria to pass and the reign of witches to end, waiting for the people to realize what a price they were paying for what they did not need, waiting for the dominant group to defeat itself by its own excesses. He believed that in the course of time nature would take its course. His mood varied, to be sure; and at moments he despaired of the future of liberty in the existing Union. In that mood he said some things, fortunately in private, which would have been better left unsaid. On the whole, however, he gives the impression of wise prudence and confident patience, though his patience is not to be confused with resignation.

He defined the issues of the time notably in some of his letters, laying down a platform for his party, but this leader does not seem to have had much to do with organization. As the crucial election year approached, it was obvious that, under the American system, the issue would have to be decided in the various states. There the congressmen were chosen by districts and the United States senators elected by legislatures, while the presidential electors were chosen as the state legislatures saw fit. These bodies could and often did change the rules so as to benefit the party in power in a particular state. Thus the crucial struggle was waged in the local legislative districts. There was no real national campaign, and Jefferson could not possibly have entered into these numerous local contests.

The success of the Republicans in the famous election of 1800 is partly attributable to better organization at the local level, and credit for this must of course be divided. Historians accord a large share of it to Aaron Burr, who procured a Republican majority in the legislature of New York, a state where under existing law presidential electors were chosen by the legislature. After these Republican successes in the spring of 1800, Hamilton suggested that the old legislature be summoned while there was yet time in order to change the provision for the choice of electors. This suggestion

Governor John Jay properly ignored. It is mentioned here chiefly by way of comparison with a change in the rules made by the General Assembly of Virginia—before the election, however—so that electors, who had been chosen by popular vote in districts in 1796, should now be chosen on a general ticket. The Republicans had failed to carry one district for Jefferson that year, and by this change they hoped to pick up all the votes, as indeed they did.

Jefferson's own judgment on this proposal was that popular election by districts was the fairest method if followed everywhere, but that since it was not followed, the change would not be improper. This was a political decision of no great moment in view of the partisan doings in other states where far greater injustices to minorities were committed, but it aroused strong protest from the Federalists. His party in the state created an effective organization for this campaign; he was kept fully informed of it, but he was not responsible for it; it was the work of his friends. He was also kept informed of developments in other states, and was on the best of terms with many leaders, but he did not create the machinery or direct the campaign anywhere.

That he would again be supported for the presidency was taken for granted by everybody, and the politics of the situation dictated that his running mate be Aaron Burr. This was because Burr had been conspicuously successful in New York and because he had been badly treated in the last presidential election. Jefferson had no direct part in the matter, but he agreed with other

Virginians that in view of what had happened previously they must make sure that Burr should get a full vote from the electors in Virginia. This considerate attitude on their part may well have contributed to the eventual tie between the two, for no close friend of Jefferson could afford to suggest that an electoral vote be withheld from Burr in any state.

Jefferson had no direct part in the campaign in 1800. During the summer, in fact, he was chiefly occupied in finishing the compilation of his manual of parliamentary practice—at just the time he was being abused as perhaps no other candidate for the presidential office has ever been. But no one can fail to be impressed by the extraordinary loyalty he commanded in his own party and the high degree of unity he had engendered in it. So far as the record goes he did virtually nothing at the time of the unexpected tie with Burr which the faulty electoral system made possible. But when the matter was referred to the House of Representatives the Republicans there gave him full and unquestioning support, while the Federalists by implacably supporting Burr showed themselves as indifferent to the obvious will of the victorious Republican party as they had been to that of the American people.

The Republicans had won the election, but it can be said with equal truth that the Federalists defeated themselves. The issue between Adams and Jefferson was not clear-cut, since the former had done all he could to remove the French issue and had finally defied the extremists in his own party. Indeed, we might say that

Adams and Jefferson between them defeated Hamilton. Though Jefferson spoke afterward of the Revolution of 1800, he minimized party conflict at the moment. In his inaugural address he made the surprising statement: "We are all republicans: we are all federalists." If we leave off the capital letters, as he did, this is not as surprising as it looks. It would not have been inaccurate for him to say that the spirit of 1776 had survived, that the counter-revolution was checked, and that, if the relatively small group of High Federalists were disregarded, the political differences between the rest of the people were relatively slight. What his country had escaped from was far more apparent, however, than what it had arrived at.

Some of the most important things Jefferson did and said are being postponed to another chapter, but even if these be included the direct part he had played in these events was far less than his enemies claimed, and less than historians have often assumed. This was partly because of circumstances, to be sure, and the same may be said of his predominantly negative approach to the problems of government in this period. This man who so loved to build with brick and mortar had had no chance to be politically constructive; he was driven by circumstance to oppose things that had gone too far, and at last had been forced into the secretiveness of which his enemies had previously accused him unfairly. The effects on him of these adjustments to circumstances were not wholly beneficial. But from the beginnings of his leadership of the opposition to his achievement of ascendancy his importance lay not so much in what he did but in what he was: a living embodiment of the spirit of 1776, an indestructible symbol of undying faith in the American experiment in self-government. "Jefferson and Liberty" rang the words of the song his triumphant supporters sang.

3

Jefferson
and Liberty

AT THE END of his official career Jefferson said that he had been forced to commit himself on the boisterous ocean of political passions by the enormities of his times. Yet, as he wistfully declared, nature intended him for the tranquil pursuits of science, by rendering them his supreme delight.[1] By science he meant knowledge, all knowledge, and beyond a doubt he pursued this with far greater satisfaction than he ever did politics. The "enormities" that he saw no choice but to combat were successive threats to human freedom. Thus the chief significance that he himself perceived in

---

[1] To Du Pont de Vemours, March 2, 1809, in Lipscomb and Berg, eds., *Writings*, XII, 258–260.

his partisan activities lay in such services as he thereby rendered to the cause of liberty. That others recognized this is suggested by the party song from which the title of this chapter comes:

> Rejoice! Columbia's sons, rejoice!
> To tyrants never bend the knee,
> But join with heart, and soul, and voice,
> For JEFFERSON and LIBERTY.

This was in 1801. Now let us turn back to 1776. Soon after the adoption of the Declaration of Independence the author of that manifesto placed on his personal seal this motto: "Rebellion to tyrants is obedience to God." History has linked his name for all time with the words "liberty" and "freedom." This would have been true if he had been lost at sea on his way back from France in 1789 and had never got home to become secretary of state and vice president and president. During the struggle for American independence he established beyond dispute his claim to the title of apostle of liberty. In the superb papers that he drew for Congress and his own state legislature he touched on every major aspect of human freedom—political, economic, religious, and intellectual. To their wondrous phrases his countrymen have never ceased to turn and one hopes they never will.

These were the words of a practicing statesman, not a closet philosopher, but to a notable degree their author had managed to keep himself above the strife of factions. He was still above it as minister to France, where his omnivorous mind feasted on Old World culture while he was performing his official duties far from those whom he was serving so faithfully and well. His stay abroad quickened his zeal for liberty, for his eyes beheld at first hand the despotism of contemporary Europe, and at length he foresaw the broadening of liberty's horizon as revolution began in France. He was by no means an uncritical observer of developments, and he was practical and flexible in the conduct of his country's business. Yet it would have been strange indeed if, at that time and in that place, he had not fallen to some extent under the spell of abstractions, under the spell of words and slogans. In his own mind he personalized, even deified, liberty. She was a goddess to be worshiped, and she could still be worshiped from a distance. Not until he came home was his devotion supremely tested in an arena where he was himself a contender, or, as he sometimes said, a gladiator. Then he fully shared liberty's ordeal. The question is, therefore, what this ordeal actually was during his years of political leadership and just what he did about it.

His career as secretary of state can be readily interpreted in terms of his continuing concern for principles he had previously pronounced and of his consistent effort to establish them. In the realm of foreign policy he sought full national independence, and his anti-British sentiments can be attributed to his belief that the British were the major obstacles to that independence. In the domestic field his own explanation to George Washington of the feud with Hamilton which was to prove eternal was that the system of his colleague "flowed from principles adverse to liberty." Though this does not take everything into account, it is far more credible than Hamilton's assertion that Jefferson was actuated by inordinate ambition. To him his party was not an end in itself, but increasingly he identified the cause of that party with the cause of freedom, while in his eyes the other party was that of potential tyranny. He oversimplified and perhaps exaggerated the issue in the 1790's, but the judiciousness which historians prize was not to be expected of him in the heat of conflict.

The conjunction of partisan considerations with those which may be called philosophical was shown clearly in his judgment on George Washington when the President denounced the democratic societies after the Whiskey Rebellion. (Jefferson himself had no direct connection with any of these societies, but they were Republican in membership.) This was during his own retirement, and it offers the first clear sign of the beginnings of a breach with one whom he had revered and whose judgment he had generally admired. Both he and Madison viewed this as an attack on their party and also on the right of free association and political dissent, objecting to it on both grounds.

Precisely the same thing was true of the Alien and Sedition Acts—especially the Sedition Act, which sought to silence criticism of the President and Congress. (There was no mention of his own office in it.) Ostensibly this was adopted for a patriotic purpose and in the name of public order. As one High Federalist said, "disorganizers" were being arrested for libeling the President and his Secretary of State "to try whether we have strength enough to cause the constituted authorities to be respected." But the real attitude of the group in power was better described by one of their supporting newspapers. This paper candidly said: "It is patriotism to write in favor of our government—it is sedition to write against it." [2] By the government, of course, the editor meant the persons then running it. Obviously the law was designed and unquestionably it was executed with a view to the suppression of a party, the legitimacy of which was denied. This sytem of suppression was a supreme challenge to Jefferson as a lifelong champion of freedom *and* as a party leader.

He saw from the beginning that the Sedition Act was directed especially against the Republican newspapers. Its advocates sought to justify it on the ground that the Republican press was scurrilous. The same charge may be made against many of the more numerous administration papers. In the history of vituperation in the United States it would be hard to match William Cobbett or Peter Porcupine, and it may be contended that in this era more outrageous things were said about Jefferson than about John Adams. If we include Jefferson's presidency, there can be no doubt of this. During his vice presidency, when he was also leader of the

---

[2] R. Troup to R. King, July 10, 1798, in C. R. King, *Life and Correspondence of Rufus King,* II (1895), 362–364; *Gazette of the United States,* October 10, 1798.

opposition, one would hesitate to say whether the pot or the kettle was the blacker. But no reader of those newspapers can deny that some of the Republican sheets were scurrilous and reckless. The editors were not always directly to blame, for there were more communications than editorials. These were commonly signed by a fictitious name, and many papers, both Federalist and Republican, accepted communications from both sides. They did this rather casually, though the editors may be pardoned for not having read all of these communications carefully, for many of them were exceptionally dull. Nonetheless, some of the most conspicuous Republican editors and pamphleteers were extremely abusive. We may properly inquire, therefore, into Jefferson's attitude toward and relations with them as a party leader.

His well-known interest in the press was thoroughly in character with the zeal for public enlightenment for which he is so justly noted. If anybody in his time believed in salvation by knowledge and information, surely he did. Throughout his entire mature life he strove to expand knowledge and diffuse information. Light and liberty go together, he said; they *must* go together. While he was in France he went so far as to declare that, if he had to choose, he would rather have newspapers without a government than a government without newspapers. This was one of those hyperboles that he allowed himself in private correspondence. The newspapers he had seen until that time warranted no such confidence. They shed only a limited amount of light, and that was often impure. What he meant was that final reliance must be placed on an informed electorate. And so far as current political issues were concerned, there was no medium of general public information except newspapers and pamphlets, which generally appeared in newspapers first.

To this statement one addition should be made: some members of Congress sought to inform their own section of the public about current issues by circular letters to their constituents. This was done on both sides. The letters of the arch-Federalist Robert Goodloe Harper of South Carolina to his constituents have long been accessible to historians in printed form, and no one can rightly deny their intolerant partisanship. But, a year before the passage of the Sedition Act, a congressman from Virginia was the object of a federal grand jury presentment because in communications to his constituents he ventured to criticize administration policy. Jefferson was much exercised about this and drafted resolutions on the subject.[3] The congressman in question was not prosecuted, but Jefferson thought that the Sedition Act might be directed at this sort of writing by Republican congressmen, while Federalist representatives were left undisturbed.

In fact, it was not so used, though one rambunctious Republican representative, Matthew Lyon of Vermont,

---

[3] This incident is described by Adrienne Koch in *Jefferson and Madison* (New York, 1950), pp. 182–184.

was convicted, among other things, for the publication of a pamphlet when Congress was not in session. The systematic campaign under the Sedition Act was against Republican newspapers, a considerable number of which were silenced. The chief enforcement officer, Secretary of State Pickering, denied that this was an attack on freedom of speech and freedom of the press. Punishment was prescribed, he said, only for "pests of society, and disturbers of peace and tranquility." John Adams was pleased with this statement. Coming from a bitter partisan like Pickering, the rationalization is unconvincing, but some of these editors and pamphleteers were indubitably pests and disturbers who went beyond the bounds of good manners and good taste, descending at times to personal abuse which served no possible public purpose. Whether or not they fell below the level of the worst Federalist writers, they fell below Jefferson's own standards as a gentleman and scholar, and at least one of them must be described as an unscrupulous scoundrel, namely, James Thomson Callender.

What did Jefferson do about them? What did he say? He consistently encouraged Republican writers, recognizing that there were none of them to spare. The tangible aid he gave them, the financial support, was in general slight. It was more than matched by the support provided Federalist editors by Hamilton. If there is any satisfaction in the fact, when one finds something dubious or bad in Jefferson he can generally find something of the same sort in Hamilton that is as bad or worse. And it seems safe to say that the pattern of political controversy in this era was set by Hamilton far more than by Jefferson. The Republican leader subscribed to party papers and commended them to others. Occasionally he contributed money, along with others, to a journal in distress, a situation in which journals tended to be at that time. But actions of this sort seem to have been greater on the part of Federalists, and they had substantial support to offer in the form of government printing. It was a distinct financial advantage to a newspaper to be on the administration side.

Jefferson's enemies often charged that he was largely responsible for what Republican editors had to say. In the House of Representatives, "Long John" Allen of Connecticut, whose fanatical zeal to extirpate imagined enemies of the Republic might entitle him to be designated as a "radical of the right," announced that the Vice President walked the streets arm-in-arm with Benjamin Franklin Bache of the Philadelphia *Aurora* and was closeted with that "infamous printer" day and night. It is impossible either to prove or disprove that Jefferson made suggestions to this journalistic gadfly, and there was no good reason why he should not have, but it is doubtful if he needed to and it would have been characteristic of him to follow a hands-off policy. He could not have handed out inside information, for at this stage he did not have it, and Bache's occasional scoops can be best attributed to his journalistic enterprise, which was perhaps excessive and certainly irresponsible.

The level of journalism was so low that Jefferson, for all his sensitiveness, may have developed a degree of im-

munity or tolerance to irresponsible statements and vitu-
perative language, whichever side they came from. This
may have been necessary for political survival at the
time. But his personal relations with Callender raise
some difficult questions. These can be considered only
briefly here.

The charge that Jefferson hired Callender to revile
Hamilton and Adams was a partisan distortion, but he
did give money to this journeyman pamphleteer. We
know this from his account book and private letters. (It
may be noted in passing that few if any of his contemporaries left so full a record and thus exposed themselves
in equal degree to the scrutiny of posterity.) He himself
described this as charity, and it may be thus regarded,
especially at the beginning. Persons in need found him
an easy mark, and Callender, who eked out a precarious
existence with his pen, was importunate. Since he had
fled England to escape prosecution for words of his
against the British King and government, Jefferson took
him at face value as a victim of persecution, and of
course he welcomed additions to the slim band of Republican writers. But his early gifts were too small and
infrequent to be significant. They did not become large
enough to amount to anything until Callender fled
Philadelphia for Virginia and regarded himself, and was
regarded by Jefferson, as the object of partisan persecution. No doubt Jefferson then felt that he could not let
him down. With others, therefore, he contributed to his
support, paying him about $150 altogether before the
election. Callender's numerous requests for aid might

be interpreted by hostile critics as a form of blackmail, and he himself was not above regarding gifts to him as payments for party services rendered, but if at this stage Jefferson had repudiated and abandoned the man, probably he would have charged himself with inhumanity.

It cannot be proved and seems most unlikely that he was directly responsible for anything that Callender wrote. He gave Callender some information, on request, when that writer was preparing *The Prospect Before Us* (Volume I, 1800), but Jefferson would have given this to anybody. He was sent some pages of this violently partisan work in advance and approved them in general terms beyond their merit, without making any specific comment. He did not suggest or expressly sanction the "calumnies and falsehoods" against John Adams at a time when he himself was the object of equally or more scurrilous attacks. But at this stage he condoned Callender's writings for what seemed to him sufficient public reasons. He appears to have done this, also, when Callender made the charge in 1797 that occasioned Hamilton to expose to public view his personal relations with Mrs. Reynolds in order to vindicate his integrity as an official. That is, Jefferson purchased Callender's pamphlet and tacitly condemned his former colleague by his own silence. He never showed any inclination to exploit the private misdeeds of his enemies: he said little or nothing anywhere about Hamilton's lapses— a subject on which John Adams afterward expressed himself with devastating candor. He was concerned with *public* conduct, and in this instance he seems to have believed that Hamilton had not really cleared himself of the public charges.[4]

At Callender's trial for sedition, during the election year of 1800, he faced High Federalism in its most arrogant, intolerant, and even brutal form in the person of Justice Samuel Chase, while he himself represented Republican journalism at its worst. Jefferson was indubitably gullible in dealing with him, and in this relationship with one whose standards were so much lower than his own the Republican leader revealed the dangers of the uncritical attitude toward the supporters of his cause which did so much to create solidarity and loyalty. For his blindness and uncritical partisanship he was to make retribution many times over: it was Callender who loosed the tongue of slander against him when he was president and did more to smear him than any other man who ever lived. These charges of personal immorality, except for one bearing on an early lapse which Jefferson privately admitted, were malicious and unwarranted.

---

[4] These involved an episode of which he had personal knowledge as secretary of state; and he was convinced at the time that Hamilton was covering up certain operations, based on inside information from somebody in the Treasury Department, from which speculators profited. There is interesting material on this topic in J. P. Boyd, ed., *Papers of Thomas Jefferson*, XVI (Princeton, 1961), 455–470, and more is promised for the next volume. The editor of that work thinks that this whole matter deserves further investigation.

The most noteworthy single action that Jefferson took in this period as a champion of individual freedom and the right of political opposition was against the Alien and Sedition Acts. In this he was obviously motivated by partisan as well as philosophical considerations; and in the resulting documents, especially the Kentucky Resolutions which he drafted, we can readily perceive evil as well as good. In the late summer of 1798, when he was back at Monticello at the end of what was perhaps the most intolerant congressional session in our history, he still believed that if war with France could be avoided nature would eventually take its course and the Federalists wreck themselves by their own excesses. Nonetheless, he believed that something could and should be done on the state level in behalf of liberty and his harassed party. That is, something could and should be *said*. Therefore, he sent to the legislature of Kentucky through a friend a set of resolutions, and he induced Madison to draft a set for Virginia, thus starting a verbal counter attack.[5] His main purpose was to make the Alien and Sedition Acts the central political issue. It seems unlikely that they became that in the public mind. The excess of the Federalists which probably did most to defeat them was the imposition of high taxes. But by pressing what he regarded as the crucial issue he left

---

[5] The best account of the drafting of these famous resolutions is that of Adrienne Koch in *Jefferson and Madison*, chapter 7. To this I am much indebted. It follows an article by the author and Harry Ammon in *William and Mary Quarterly* (April, 1948).

an indelible mark on the pages of our history and did much to cast upon these repressive measures the opprobrium they still rightly bear.

The procedure he followed in this instance was in line with what was now standard practice on the part of the Republican leaders in his state. They began it about five years earlier, taking their cue from Hamilton, who, at the time of Genet, instigated various merchant groups in commerical centers to adopt adddresses and resolutions which were patriotic in form but also supported his own interpretation of neutrality. After Jefferson had given wise private counsel about desirable Republican policy, Madison and others drafted resolutions which were adopted in a somewhat variant form in certain counties of Virginia. Jefferson and Madison now framed resolutions for adoption by state legislatures, and if the author was not a member of the legislature or even a resident of the state it was natural that his identity should be unrevealed. Since there were other compelling reasons why Jefferson wanted his name unmentioned, his secretive procedure is understandable. More surprising is the fact that his authorship of the Kentucky Resolutions did not come to public knowledge until long after he had retired from public life.

Jefferson's Kentucky Resolutions, which were shrouded in such secrecy, present many difficulties of interpretation. The chief one is that this document and the others in the series it initiated have a dual character and significance. They are human-rights documents, but also they set forth the current Republican doctrine of state rights. Hence one must make a choice of emphasis. A further difficulty arises from the fact that, as statements of a constitutional position, they are not in entire accord. Jefferson took the most extreme position at the outset. Madison, closing the series in his Report of early 1800 to the Virginia General Assembly, presented the Republican constitutional position in its fullest, most closely reasoned, most carefully qualified and safeguarded, and therefore in its most tenable form.[6]

Did Jefferson himself recede to this more defensible position? Despite the shroud of secrecy in which he had enveloped himself, we may assume that he did. He generally yielded to Madison's judgment in constitutional matters when it was firmly presented, and never again did he say or imply that an act of the federal government was unconstitutional because the legislature of a single state declared it so. Nor did he again suggest that a single state might nullify such a law within its own borders, as he did in the draft of resolutions he sent to Kentucky in 1798. (Ironically, the Kentuckians left it out that year, but put it into the resolutions they adopted the next year—resolutions which were not written by Jefferson. It is also ironical that as President he himself had to contend with nullification in New England.) These suggestions went farther in the state-rights direction than any others he ever made. One can

---

[6] The series consisted of the Kentucky Resolutions of 1798, the Virginia Resolutions of 1798, the Kentucky Resolutions of 1799, and Madison's Report of 1800.

believe that if Madison had seen the Kentucky Resolutions before they were dispatched, he would have talked Jefferson into leaving out the most extreme suggestions in the first place.

This brings to mind an illuminating comment of Madison's in old age: namely, that allowance must be made for "a habit in Mr. Jefferson as in others of great genius of expressing in strong and round terms, impressions of the moment." [7] Mr. Jefferson, who was so much on his guard in public, blew off steam in private to relieve the pressure. The exaggeration which he permitted himself in private communication, somewhat to the embarrassment of his later interpreters, probably contributed to his contemporary effectiveness as a catalytic agent. He stimulated his supporters in a way that Madison could never do. But, after throwing out a hasty proposal, he was disposed to accept with little protest the judgment of trusted friends that it was impracticable or unwise. His letters in this period show unmistakably that what he most wanted to avoid was overt action, being convinced that this would be disastrous. He therefore raised no objection when John Breckinridge of Kentucky threw out his reference to nullification. No doubt he now recognized that it was not a good idea. For the same reason he accepted Madison's veto of his later suggestion that reference be made in the second set of Kentucky Resolutions to the theo-

---

[7] To N. P. Trist, May, 1832, in Gaillard Hunt, ed., *Writings of James Madison*, IX (1910), 479.

retical right of secession. The suggestion was not as shocking as it would have seemed a generation or two later, but a major contemporary criticism of this series of resolutions was that they were disunionist in trend, and there was no point in talking about an ultimate right when he had no thought of resorting to it. The emphasis belonged where Madison put it: that is, on preserving the Union by preventing the abuse of federal power and keeping the government in balance.

The Kentucky Resolutions of 1798 constitute no well-rounded and well-balanced treatise on federal relations, such as Madison's Report of 1800 does. This was an *ad hoc* document, addressed to a particular situation. Its primary purpose was to start a wave of protest against infringements on human liberty and against the denial of the right of political opposition. The present actuality was that freedom of expression and the very existence of his party, which was to his mind the party of freedom, were gravely threatened. Threatened by whom? By the general government. And if he had not turned to the states for their protection at this time, whither could he have turned? There would have been no point in appealing to the Supreme Court of the United States. That partisan body was no guardian of the rights of individuals, as the Supreme Court is today. At the time the federal judiciary was guarding the group then in power and it left on the pages of history an ineffaceable image of intolerance.

That is, Jefferson invoked state rights in behalf of human rights. He did not invoke them *against* human rights or in behalf of vested local interests; nor did he emphasize them for their own sake. They were merely a means to an end, just as all political institutions were to him, including the Union itself. Throughout his career thus far his thought and interest had always centered on the individual. Actually he said little about the rights of states until he tangled with Hamilton and became alarmed by his colleague's consolidating proclivities. Supremely, he was an individualist.

Even at this distance it is easy to see why he feared the general government as an actual or potential threat to the freedom of individual human beings. It is harder to understand why he was, or seemed, much less fearful of the governments of states. The explanation lies partly in his confidence in his own commonwealth, which had a tradition of tolerance, and where his own party, which he regarded as the party of freedom, was in firm control. But his eyes were not on Virginia alone when he voiced his faith at this and a later time. In a letter of his old age to a French philosopher he described the state governments as the true protectors of liberty and as "the wisest conservative power ever contrived by man." [8] There were seventeen of them by then, and because of their number and geographical dispersion, he believed that they would never *all* yield to usurpation or despotism. In his age, transportation and communication were slower than we can easily imagine, and he was still talk-

---

[8] To Destutt de Tracy, January 26, 1811, in Ford, *Writings,* IX, 308–309.

ing as though the greatest danger to be avoided was the rule of a single tyrant. He never could escape his phobia about kings. But what he had in mind was the blessings of diversity and the safety which inheres in it. Some states might be tyrannical, but it was not to be expected that all would be.

Thus he believed that human liberties stood a better chance at the hands of the states than at those of the general government, and, according to the constitutional theory at which he had arrived, that was where human liberties were. He recognized that state governments could legally curtail some of them. In his draft of the Kentucky Resolutions he said that the states had retained for themselves "the right of judging how far licentiousness of speech and of the press may be abridged without lessening their useful freedom." A score of years before this, he had written in his justly famous bill for establishing religious freedom "that the opinions of men are not the object of civil government, nor under its jurisdiction." The fact that the Virginia legislature deleted this before passing the bill strongly suggests that he was in advance of prevailing sentiment, but there is no reason to suppose that he had receded from this position. He had already said and was to repeat in his first inaugural address that errors may be tolerated when reason is left free to combat them. Also, he had said that civil government should limit its concern to overt acts. That was the ideal, certainly, but even at this stage, when he was so vigorously defending the freedom of the press, he does not seem to have regarded that freedom as an absolute or to have thought all government powerless to restrain its licentiousness. He consistently took the position that a state had the legal right to abridge its freedom. He repeated this after he became president, when he also said that the occasional punishment of outrageous libel was salutary.

It is in this light that the relatively few actions against libel during his own presidency should be viewed. The only one of these that he is believed to have expressly encouraged, a state action in Pennsylvania, was directed against an editor who denounced the democratic form of government and thus attacked the basic doctrine of the sovereignty of the people on which we have built our whole political system.[9] He did little about the torrent of personal slander against himself, which far exceeded anything John Adams had to endure, though on several occasions he departed from his previous policy of not writing anonymously for the newspapers. Some of his followers, in a punitive spirit, did things which were inconsistent with the preachments of their party, and it is regrettable that he did not do more to discourage them. But there were relatively few cases of the sort. There was no campaign of persecution, no concerted

---

[9] The case was that of Joseph Dennie, charged with libel in the *Port Folio* (April 23, 1803); 4 Yeates' (Pa.) *Reports* (1805), 266–267. See Jefferson to Governor Thos. McKean, February 19, 1803, in *Writings*, VIII, 218. In *Legacy of Suppression* (Cambridge, Mass.; 1960), pp. 297–307, Leonard W. Levy takes a more unfavorable view of the libel cases of Jefferson's administration than I do when viewing them in their full context.

attempt to destroy the opposition, as there had been during the ascendancy of High Federalism, when all branches of the general government joined in. Some of his implacable foes claimed that he instituted a reign of terror, but this was absurd.

It would be foolish to assert that Jefferson, when bearing the responsibilities of the first office, had precisely the same feeling about criticism as when he was in opposition. We have no right to expect that of any man. No human being is wholly fair-minded or wholly just, but some are much more so than others, and everybody must be judged at last on balance. Every historical character must also be judged in his own setting of time and circumstance. Jefferson was a fallible mortal and by no means incapable of self-deception and rationalization. But nobody who has lived with him through his problems day by day can believe that amid the tribulations of his presidency he ceased to be a devoted friend to freedom. If the generation that then began did not mark the heyday of American individualism, what generation ever did?

The period of his active party leadership was not the portion of his long and extraordinarily distinguished career on which his own memory most fondly dwelled When he himself selected, for inscription on his tombstone, those achievements by which he most wanted to be remembered, he turned to the early morning of our country's history, when he heralded its freedom of body and of spirit, and to his own twilight, when he crowned a lifetime of service to human enlightenment by fathering a university. As his correspondence with John Adams clearly shows, he did not like to recall the heat, the sweat, the bitter strife of midday. And it is harder to understand him as a party leader than as a prophet and a sage.

As such he was to some extent an opportunist, and he could not keep his mind focused at all times on the eternal verities. But it was in the midst of his most crucial political struggle that he said some of the noblest and most characteristic things he ever said. The year after he penned the Kentucky Resolutions he wrote to a student at the College of William and Mary that "while the art of printing is left to us, science can never be retrograde; what is once acquired of real knowledge can never be lost." In this wonderful letter he showed unmistakably that he was waging a more than defensive fight; throughout his career he had been seeking to arrest the course of despotism so that human society might be free to realize upon its immeasurable possibilities. "To preserve the freedom of the human mind then and freedom of the press," he said, "every spirit should be ready to devote itself to martyrdom; for as long as we may think as we will, and speak as we think the condition of man will proceed in improvement." [10] The improvement he envisioned was not infinite, but it was illimitable. In the heat of the campaign, again a prophet spoke.

---

[10] To William Green Munford, June 18, 1799; quoted in Koch, *Jefferson and Madison*, pp. 181–182.

In the election year of 1800, when the Republican chieftain, who was also the author of the Virginia Bill for Establishing Religious Freedom, was being attacked with unexampled bitterness as an unbeliever, he wrote the words which characterize his purposes better, probably, than any others that he ever spoke. They are now emblazoned on the walls of the memorial to him in Washington, but it was in a private letter to Dr. Benjamin Rush that he made his unforgettable personal declaration: "I have sworn upon the altar of God eternal hostility against every form of tyranny over the mind of man." [11] The now-familiar words may be repeated here as a reminder of the time he used them. But this is no partisan utterance for its own day only. Thus spoke a champion of the freedom on which depend all other freedoms and the progress of mankind. What other political leader in our history or any other history ever did more to liberate and safeguard man's immortal mind?

---

[11] September 23, 1800; *Writings*, VII, 460.

Index